Winning Shopping Center Designs

No. 8

Visual Reference Publications, New York

Visual Reference Publications, Inc.
302 Fifth Avenue
New York, NY 10001

Distributors to the trade in the United States and Canada
Watson-Guptill Publications
770 Broadway
New York, NY 10003

Distributors outside the United States and Canada
HarperCollins International
10 East 53rd Street
New York, NY 10022

Library of Congress Cataloging in Publication Data:
Winning Shopping Center Designs No. 8

Printed in China
ISBN 1-58471-059-4

Book Design: Harish Patel Design Associates, New York

Contents

About the ICSC International Design and Development Awards

The ICSC International Design and Development Awards Program was established to recognize outstanding shopping center projects and to provide information on them to the entire industry so that others may benefit from the experiences of their colleagues.

The 25th International Design and Development Awards Program was worldwide in scope. Participation in other ICSC design awards programs, such as the Canadian or European awards, did not preclude eligible projects from being considered for an International Design and Development Award.

Projects that opened within the 18-month period, January 1, 1999, to June 30, 2000, were eligible for entry into this year's Awards Program.

Awards Categories

Categories for entries were:

Category A—Renovation or Expansion of an Existing Project
Entries had to relate to a project involving an entire shopping center, such as an enclosure, or a single facet of a center, such as an addition. The renovation or expansion must have been completed and the center fully opened for business within the 18-month period, January 1, 1999, to June 30, 2000. Eligible subject matter included, but was not limited to, improving the use of existing space, methods of keeping a center open during construction, new marketing and re-leasing approaches, refinancing techniques, innovative design and construction approaches, and adaptive reuse of the structure.

Category B—Innovative Design and Construction of a New Project
Entries had to relate to a specific new shopping center, completed and opened within the 18-month period, January 1, 1999, to June 30, 2000, and must have demonstrated how a specific design or construction problem was solved or how new standards in design or construction were established. New methods of environmental enhancement, space utilization design themes, energy conservation and innovative construction techniques were among the subjects that were considered for this category. Entries included detailed information about the

design and construction of the center, such as explanations of the reasons for, and the realized accomplishments of, the particular approach.

Awards Classifications

Entries submitted for either **category** were judged according to the following center **classification** system:

1. Projects under 150,000 square feet of total retail space*

2. Projects of 150,001 to 500,000 square feet of total retail space*

3. Projects over 500,001 square feet of total retail space.*

*Total retail space includes all square footage included in gross leasable areas (GLA), all department store or other anchor square footage, movie theaters, ice skating rinks, entertainment centers, and all peripheral (out-lot) space engaged in retail enterprise. It does not include office or hotel square footage.

Eligibility

1. The ICSC International Design and Development Awards Program was open only to ICSC member companies. Any ICSC member company could enter as many projects as desired in either of the two categories.

2. Entries must have had the authorization and signature of the owner or management company of the property.

3. Projects opened within the 18-month period, January 1, 1999 to June 30, 2000, were eligible.

4. Projects must have been completed and opened for business by June 30, 2000.

5. Separate phases of a project could be submitted individually, provided they were completed and opened for business by June 30, 2000.

6. Projects could only be submitted once. Projects that were entered in the past could not be resubmitted unless substantial changes were made since the last submission.

7. Members entering the ICSC Canadian or ICSC European awards programs had to submit separately to the International Design and Development Awards Program, and entries had to adhere to its entry guidelines and requirements. Entries accepted into other ICSC awards programs did not automatically qualify for this program, nor was any entry excluded simply because it was an award winner in another program.

If you have any questions about the International Council of Shopping Centers International Design and Development Awards, or would like to receive an application for the upcoming awards program, please contact:

International Council of Shopping Centers International Design and Development Awards

Foreword

There were fifty entries in this year's 25th International Design and Development Awards Program. Today's shopping center industry is more international than ever before.

The emerging retail economies of eastern Europe, Asia, Africa, the middle east, and Latin America are developing excellent "leading edge" examples of both enclosed shopping malls and specialty theme centers for a growing consumer base eager to enjoy modern shopping formats. Developers in these markets have frequently combined time-proven design elements used throughout the world with distinctive features that reflect the local heritage, architecture, or lifestyle.

Many of the mature shopping center industries of the U.S., Canada, Australia, Japan, and western Europe face the equally daunting challenges of creating new retail excitement for the sensory-overloaded consumer who has dwindling time to shop. In some markets, past over-building of retail space combined with shifting demographics and retailer consolidation has resulted in the need to "de-mall" or otherwise redevelop major shopping centers. In other markets, developers and retailers have pursued unique shopping environments to give them a competitive advantage over more mundane retail presentations.

The worldwide recognition of outstanding projects forms the basis of the ICSC International Design and Development Awards Program. ICSC's historic standard of excellence was reflected this year in the five Design Award winners and fifteen Certificate of Merit recipients.

New development winners (Innovative Design and Construction of a New Project) included a 3-level mall created inside the historic shell of a 100-year-old steam train factory in former East Berlin, a small but powerful specialty center at a key Tokyo intersection, a 4-level entertainment complex in downtown Denver, and a regional center created as a redevelopment of downtown Spokane.

Winners in the Renovation or Expansion of an Existing Project category included major expansions to two very successful shopping centers: Ala Moana in Honolulu and Chadstone in Melbourne. There were other winners from the United States, South Africa and The Philippines.

The International Design and Development Awards Jury Committee was expanded this year to include eleven industry leaders from development, retailing, architecture, financial investment, and consulting firms. They average in excess of 20 years' experience each and invest many hours in judging each year's submissions. am very grateful to them for their dedication and professionalism.

This book presents the winning submissions in this year's International Design and Development Awards Program in its 25th year. We thank the entrants for their creativity, resourcefulness, and hard work. We hope this recognition inspires future projects providing world-class shopping and entertainment experiences.

Daryl K. Mangan
Chairman
ICSC 2001 International Design and Development Awards
Jury Committee

Acknowledgments

The International Council of Shopping Centers 25th International Design and Development Awards were selected by a committee of diverse shopping center professionals representing retailers, developers and architects. The International Council of Shopping Centers is grateful to these judges for the time, effort and expertise they contributed to the awards program.

Daryl K. Mangan, *Chairman*
Moreland Hills, Ohio

Ronald A. Altoon, FAIA
Altoon + Porter Architects
Los Angeles, California

Stanley C. Burgess
The Rouse Company
Columbia, Maryland

F. Carl Dieterle, Jr.
Simon Property Group
Indianapolis, Indiana

Gordon T. Greeby
GCI-ProNet Midwest
Lake Bluff, Illinois

John M. Millar, SCSM
Jones Lang LaSalle
Atlanta, Georgia

Jeffrey Olson
PaineWebber, Inc.
New York, New York

J. Thomas Porter
Thompson, Ventulett, Stainback & Associates
Atlanta, Georgia

Rao K. Sunku
J.C. Penney Co., Inc.
Dallas, Texas

Ian F. Thomas
Thomas Consultants, Inc.
Vancouver, British Columbia

Gerald M. White
Copaken, White & Blitt
Leawood, Kansas

Owner:

Denver Pavilions, L. P.
Denver, Colorado, United States

Management Company:

Entertainment Development Group
Agoura Hills, California, United States

Architect/Designer:

ELS Architecture and Urban Design
Berkeley, California, United States

General Contractor:

Hensel Phelps Construction Company
Greeley, Colorado, United States

Denver Pavilions
Denver, Colorado, United States

Gross size of center:
398,421 sq. ft.

Gross leasable area excluding anchors:
346,063 sq. ft.

Total acreage of site:
3.21 acres

Type of center:
Fashion/Specialty Center/Entertainment

Physical description:
Open mall

Location of trading area:
Urban Central Business District

Population:
- Primary trading area
  500,000

- Secondary trading area
  1,500,000

- Annualized percentage of shoppers
  anticipated to be from outside trade area
  40%

Development schedule:
- Original opening date
  July 30, 1999

Parking spaces:
- Present number
  1,000

Innovative Design and Construction of a New Project

*T*he Denver Pavilions is a new open-air retail and entertainment center in downtown Denver's business district. It spans two city blocks on a major pedestrian/ transit mall and has become a regional destination for residents, office workers, tourists and conventioneers.

The Pavilions in Denver occupy two blockfronts within a pedestrian mall.

The Pavilions has a busy look at street level.

Photos: Timothy Hursley

Old-style roof moldings tie the Pavilions' design to neighboring streets.

"Denver" is spelled out in 30-foot letters on "The Great Wall," which was developed in response to a requirement for public art within publicly funded construction.

Retailing at the Pavilions takes place at many levels.

Photos: Andrew Kramer (above and top); Timothy Hursley (left and opposite)

The complex is leasable on four levels and incorporates a multi-screen cinema, restaurants, nightclubs and small shops. Each of the two 266-foot blockfronts now contains a mid-block arcade. The arcades are connected by a multi-level bridge, and together they triple the retail frontage that would have been available with just a blockfront layout. The arcades also create distinct identities for the center's mini-anchors. The center includes two levels of garage parking that accommodate 800 cars. Shoppers can also use over 7,500 nearby office building parking spaces on weekends and evenings.

MAJOR TENANTS		
NAME	TYPE	GLA (SQ. FT.)
United Artists	Multi-screen theater	80,000
Jillian's	Entertainment and dining	32,000
Niketown	Sports apparel	30,000
Barnes & Noble	Books	27,000
Virgin Megastore	Music	25,000

The 14-screen cinema is just one of several entertainment venues within the Pavilions.

Designers sought an open-air layout for the Pavilions, in keeping with its role as a community center.

Photos: Timothy Hursley

Landscaping brings respite to the lively downtown scene.

The project was partially funded through public monies, which carried a requirement of public art. The result is "The Great Wall," a 360-foot-long, 30-foot-high artwork consisting of a perforated metal scrim screen that shows computerized light shows. "Denver" is spelled out in 30-foot letters. "The Great Wall" has been hailed as a civic icon.

The design itself is as eclectic as the community the center serves. Traditional roof crowns and awnings share space with neon and roofline-piercing signage. Colors tend toward the brick, gray and off-white of neighboring streets.

The center's facades blend seamlessly with the nearby hotels, office buildings and convention center.

There is something for the eye everywhere within the Pavilions.

At one with the design and tenants, the location has made the Pavilions the number-one downtown destination. The land it occupies was once known as the dark end of downtown, a location of many vacant storefronts. Now, the Pavilions and nearby major hotels, office buildings and the city convention center have reenergized the area.

The developer encourages others not to underestimate the difficulty of selling a prototype project like this to tenants and lenders. The result, however, is a new downtown for Denver, and retailers — particularly apparel stores — that were unable to lease space at the center are already moving to locations adjacent to the Pavilions.

Owner:
Takenaka Realty Co., Ltd.
Tokyo, Japan

Management Company:
Takenaka Corporation
Tokyo, Japan

Architect/Designer:
Takenaka Corporation
Tokyo, Japan

General Contractor:
Takenaka Corporation
Tokyo, Japan

t's harajuku
Tokyo, Japan

Gross size of center:
56,036 sq. ft.

Gross leasable area excluding anchors:
40,305 sq. ft.

Total acreage of site:
0.5 acres

Type of center:
Fashion/specialty center

Physical description:
Four-level free-standing center

Location of trading area:
Urban

Population:
• Primary trading area
  1,880,000

• Secondary trading area
  10,000,000

• Annualized percentage of shoppers
  anticipated to be from outside trade area
  15%

Development schedule:
• Original opening date
  November 3, 1999

Parking spaces:
• Present number
  28

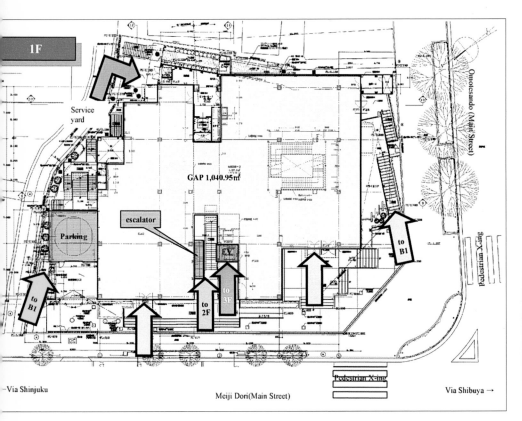

*T*he location of a new mall in downtown Tokyo presented its developers with unusual challenges and solutions. The intersection where the center lies is one of the busiest in the city. On one side, the site marks the southern boundary of what is widely regarded as the fashion center of Tokyo; on the other is a high-end retail district. And the neighborhood — described by the developer as "ultra-trendy" — evolves continuously.

The result — t's harajuku — is a four-level center mixing apparel, other retailers and eateries. Stores were deliberately chosen to represent west and east, young and old, as well as traditional Japan and modern internationalism.

The center itself serves as a billboard, giving all tenants street visibility.

The developers decided, in deference to the evolving neighborhood, to give the building a 10-year life cycle. At the end of 10 years, the building and its concept will be reevaluated and either renovated and re-leased or demolished and rebuilt.

A major concern for this vertical center — ensuring that each shop had direct street access — was achieved by a design concept allowing access to each shop without passing through other stores. By choosing to build only three floors above ground and giving all tenants equal signage

MAJOR TENANTS

NAME	TYPE	GLA (SQ. FT.)
Gap	Apparel	26,080
Elephant Café	Ethnic restaurant	5,919
PizzaExpress	Pizza restaurant	3,613
Sony Plaza	Character, accessory goods	3,570
Den	Japanese-style dining bar	1,123

Clear glass denotes retail floors, while a corrugated "skin" identifies eatery levels.

Gap (above) uses video screens to entertain and inform shoppers using the staircase in the central atrium.

*The Elephant Café
(left) presents pan-
Asian design and
cuisine. Use of
lighting for interior
space (below) opens up
a tight passageway.*

and access, the developer has created a balance among the retailers without disenfranchising upper-floor tenants.

Balance and visual unity also result from using the building itself as a billboard device for all tenants. The billboard is flush with the building, creating a unified design. The exterior design focuses on simplicity, using transparent glass so that retailers can promote their wares. A corrugated "skin" distinguishes the lower retail floors from the upper restaurant section of the building.

Tenant opening schedules and other timing issues led to a decision to use the basement walls and slabs of an earlier building (completed in 1958) for the new center; this also reduced construction costs considerably. Despite the building's planned 10-year life span, it has been built to withstand seismic activity to the same degree as any permanent structure.

The Den (left) features a traditional Japanese dining experience. Sony Plaza (below) focuses on imported goods.

The center's retail mix reflects the demographics of its customers. The neighborhood trend toward the young — represented by the domestically popular Sony Plaza and Elephant Café — has been balanced with Gap, PizzaExpress and Den, which appeal to customers in their 30s and 40s. This bringing together of people is bolstered by the building's setback from the street, providing an area where people can congregate — a rarity in the neighborhood. Based on the success of t's harajuku, its developers were asked to participate in the new development on an adjacent site.

*Design at
t's harajuku
incorporates
textures, colors and
a wide variety of
lighting treatments.*

Certificate of Merit

Owner and Management Company
Cousins MarketCenters, Inc.
Atlanta, Georgia, United States

Architect/Designer:
Crawford McWilliams Hatcher Architects, Inc.
Birmingham, Alabama, United States

General Contractor:
Hardin Construction Group, Inc.
Atlanta, Georgia, United States

The Avenue East Cobb
Marietta, Georgia, United States

Gross size of center:
243,278 sq. ft.

Gross leasable area excluding anchors:
224,494 sq. ft.

Total acreage of site:
30.97 acres

Type of center:
Fashion/specialty center

Physical description:
Lifestyle center

Location of trading area:
Suburban

Population:
- Primary trading area
  172,104

- Secondary trading area
  163,209

- Annualized percentage of shoppers
  anticipated to be from outside trade area
  10%

Development schedule:
- Opening date
  August 12, 1999

Parking spaces:
- Present number
  1,171

The U-shaped layout of the Avenue East Cobb offers high visibility for all storefronts.

*T*he Avenue East Cobb in Marietta, Georgia, combines retailing with a sense of traditional Southern downtown design. National retailers, select local merchants and specialty restaurants wrap around a U-shaped layout.

Bronze sculptures and cast-iron lampposts reinforce the Southern downtown style of the center.

The developer and architect decided that the upscale nature of the project merited storefronts more elaborate than are usually found in open-air centers. They created a project tenant criteria manual that listed approved building materials, defined tenant work areas and gave illustrations of signage and architectural details that would be appropriate to the design plans. A tenant coordinator helped the stores submit exterior designs that would meet with the approval of the developer and designer.

Main Street-style storefronts, plaza-like brick pavers, cast-iron lampposts and sconces, fountains, small-paned windows, benches and landscaping create the sense of Southern downtown that the developers knew would attract customers. Design enhancements include 11 bronze sculptures placed along the sidewalks, exterior moldings, plaster inlays in the brick walls and various textures in the brick pavers.

Eleven types of brick pavers and seating areas give an upscale look to the community center.

The center offers an abundance of seating areas and walkways outdoors.

The U-shaped site plan serves the retailers well, making storefronts visible from one another and giving each store roughly equal attraction to passing shoppers. A raised, brick-paved and landscaped sidewalk cuts across the U-shaped parking lot, reinforcing the people-friendly aspect of the center. Speed bumps slow traffic and increase shopper safety. More than 200 feet separate the nearest stores from the main entrance.

No store in the center is larger than 25,000 square feet, reflecting the small-town community focus of the Avenue East Cobb.

MAJOR TENANTS		
NAME	**TYPE**	**GLA (SQ. FT.)**
Borders Books & Music	Book and music store	24,900
Bed Bath & Beyond	Home store	21,000
Gap Concepts	Lifestyle clothier	19,400

Extensive landscaping breaks up the brickwork and provides shade in the Georgia summer.

A youngster finds two bronzed playmates at the Avenue East Cobb.

Photos: CMH Architects, Inc.

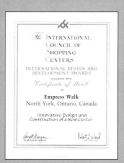

Owner:

Riocan (Empress Walk) Holdings Inc.
Toronto, Ontario, Canada

Management Company:

Menkes Property Management Services Ltd.
Toronto, Ontario, Canada

Architect:

Page & Steele Architects
Toronto, Ontario, Canada

Designer:

D. I. Design & Development Consultants Limited
Toronto, Ontario, Canada

General Contractor:

Eastern Construction
Toronto, Ontario, Canada

Empress Walk
North York, Ontario, Canada

Gross size of center:
241,791 sq. ft.

Gross leasable area excluding anchors:
118,047 sq. ft.

Total acreage of site:
3.16 acres

Type of center:
Community, theme/festival center

Physical description:
Four-story enclosed mall

Location of trading area:
Urban but not downtown

Population:
• Primary trading area
  254,000

• Secondary trading area
  407,000

Development schedule:
• Original opening date
  November 1999

Parking spaces:
• Present number
  791

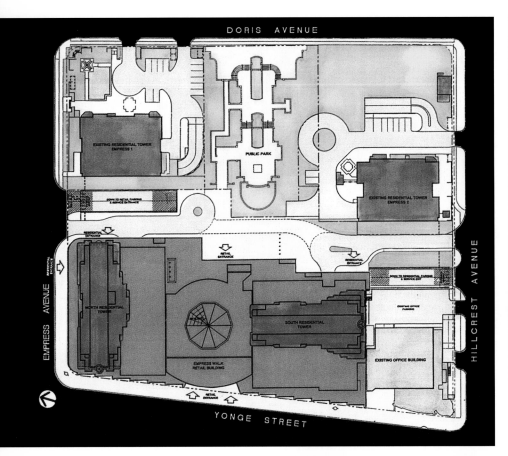

E mpress Walk, in the North York suburb of Toronto, is a four-level retail and entertainment center featuring an atrium, 10-screen cinema, upscale food store, entertainment retailers and restaurants. With two 33-story residential condominium towers, Empress Walk forms the second phase of a two-part development, following two other residential towers. The center is on Toronto's principal retail street, directly opposite a major municipal office building, public library, park and performing arts theater.

Empress Walk (lower left of the site map) is a four-floor retail atrium at the base of two residential towers. At left, lighted signs draw shoppers to Empress Walk.

The two new towers (above) created structural challenges for the retail and cinema space. Lots of glass (right) and a red neon beacon encourage passersby to spend time in this urban retail/entertainment center.

MAJOR TENANTS		
NAME	**TYPE**	**GLA (SQ. FT.)**
Famous Players	Multi-screen theater	63,644
Loblaws	Supermarket	60,100
Indigo Books & Music	Book and music store	25,858
Tower Records	Music store	16,906

Animated lighting around the building's perimeter (left) distinguishes Empress Walk at night. Below, a continuous undulating open metal screening device hides the rear walls of the upper-level cinemas. At night, the device is used as a screen for projections and animated lighting.

The main challenge of building Empress Walk was the design of the structural transfer system, which would enable the 33-story residential concrete tower walls and lateral loads to be safely transmitted through the cinema level of the center. The theaters' layout would not permit any columns or walls within the seating areas. The solution was to use the floor directly above the cinema level as a transfer floor consisting of 15-foot-high, floor-to-floor concrete wall beams, which measure 24 inches thick and span 62 feet.

The multi-level retail space under the atrium contains the 10-screen cinema on the upper level and entertainment-focused retailers on the lower levels.

To withstand wind and earthquake forces at the cinema level, concrete walls were introduced around the perimeter of the cinema, forming a box. These walls support the wall beams and provide lateral rigidity for the towers above. Below the cinema level, the box wall is supported by concrete columns, which extend down through the retail floors and five levels of sub-grade space. Due to cinema space constraints, the box walls were limited to a thickness of 18 inches and a height of 46 feet. This combination of tall unsupported height and high loads from the tower necessitated use of high-strength 65 MPs concrete and a heavy reinforcing steel percentage.

Strong patterns in floors and ceilings distinguish the interior design.

To prevent cinema sounds and vibrations from transmitting to the residential floors above, the cinema seat stadia structure was isolated from the base building structure by floating acoustics-bearing pads. Essentially, the cinema is floating free with no direct contact to the outside walls except though these floating pads.

Both the storefronts and the merchandise within have strong visual impact.

Primary colors are used as bold accents under the atrium at Empress Walk.

Empress Walk's retailers were chosen with an eye to the nearby tower residents as well as people seeking lifestyle retailers and restaurants. Combined with the cinema and a one-acre public park donated from private sources, Empress Walk embraces a wide range of customers and needs, creating a landmark gathering place in a busy urban center.

Certificate of Merit

Owner:
DEGI Deutsche Gesellschaft für Immobilienfonds mbH
Frankfurt, Germany

Management Company:
RSE Service GmbH
Berlin, Germany

Architect/Designer:
Claude Vasconi/Dagmar Gross
Paris, France

Hallen Am Borsigturm
Berlin, Germany

Gross size of center:
530,000 sq. ft.

Gross leasable area excluding anchors:
195,000 sq. ft.

Total acreage of site:
9.64 acres

Type of center:
Regional center

Physical description:
Enclosed three-level mall

Location of trading area:
Urban but not downtown

Population:
- Primary trading area
  136,000

- Secondary trading area
  209,000

- Annualized percentage of shoppers anticipated to be from outside trade area
  20%

Development schedule:
- Original opening date
  March 25,1999

Parking spaces:
- Present number
  1,600

A former locomotive production facility in the northern section of Berlin had become an industrial wasteland by the early 1990s. The few surviving brick structures, while impressive, were threatened with decay. The area, however, has excellent links to the city's transportation system by car, bus and rail; Berlin's Tegel Airport is only minutes away. The area was also lacking in retail — 8.3 square feet per person, compared to a Berlin-wide average of 11.6 square feet — resulting in an annual outflow of $285 million in purchasing power.

The northward entrance has a modern, dynamically designed glass facade.

The historic value of the former locomotive production halls (above and below) are evident in the new Hallen Am Borsigturm shopping center.

MAJOR TENANTS		
NAME	TYPE	GLA (SQ. FT.)
Real	Department store	88,000
CineStar	Multi-screen theater	55,000
Media Markt	Electronics	35,000
Healthland Fitness	Fitness	27,000
Hennes & Mauritz	Textiles	25,000
Kaiser's	Food	24,000
Bowling Center	Sports	24,000

The new food court (above) has clear visual ties to the old locomotive facility (above, left). The brick entryways (left) lend a sense of history to modern glass and steel.

To capitalize on this need, the developers of Hallen Am Borsigturm designed a new facility combining retail, leisure activity, a fitness facility, bowling alley, discotheque, movie theaters and restaurants. The developer and architects agreed that the surviving production facilities should be preserved, making their incorporation into the retail/entertainment facility the project's primary goal.

Retailers have found imaginative ways to come to terms with the steel structure of the expanded mall.

Hallen Am Borsigturm is integrated into five former locomotive construction halls. Historically rich facades were preserved, as was the entire internal steel structure of the halls. The structural system of the new retail area was also based on the historic elements. The newly built middle hall in the historic line of buildings at the southern side works with two old facade gables in the new building on the eastern side to form a harmonious

Tenants' logos (above) draw shoppers from a distance. Entry into the multi-level parking lot (right) is aided by extensive signage (above, right).

Indoor walkways and bridges help make Hallen Am Borsigturm a thriving retail environment.

dialogue between the preserved and new elements. Integration of the historical steel pillars in the tenants' areas proved difficult, since retailers are used to standardized mall structures, but mutually advantageous solutions were found.

The combination of leisure and retail facilities was particularly beneficial to the tenants. Since the main hall is open beyond stores' operating hours, visitors to the leisure level take the opportunity to window-shop on weekends and in the evenings. Weekend window-shopping means that Mondays — a day when trade is normally slow — have turned into an excellent shopping day for the center's stores.

Hallen Am Borsigturm also serves as a community center, hosting such events as the Berlin Symphonic Orchestra's Millennium Concert. The developer and designer believe the Hallen Am Borsigturm offers a fine example of the successful integration of historic architecture into modern retail settings.

Over 7 million people visited Hallen Am Borsigturm during its first year, attracted by the combination of retail, entertainment and history.

Owner:
Cancun Walk, S. A. de C. V.
Mexico City, D. F., Mexico

Management Company:
Condominio Isla Cancun, A. C.
Mexico City, D. F., Mexico

Architect/Designer:
GICSA Proyectos
Mexico City, D. F., Mexico

General Contractor:
Construcabi
Mexico City, D. F., Mexico

La Isla
Shopping Village
Cancun, Quintana Roo, Mexico

Gross size of center:
545,104 sq. ft.

Gross leasable area excluding anchors:
274,202 sq. ft.

Total acreage of site:
17 acres

Type of center:
Super-regional, theme/festival center

Physical description:
Open one-level mall

Location of trading area:
Tourist hotel strip

Population:
• Annualized percentage of shoppers anticipated to be from outside trade area 90%

Development schedule:
• Original opening date October 1999

Parking spaces:
• Present number 710

• 440 parking spaces to be added

A rich array of restaurants, cinemas and an interactive aquarium comprise La Isla Shopping Village in Cancun, Mexico. Tourism brings in 90 percent of its shoppers, who are drawn to the center's Mexican Caribbean theme and open-air "island" ambiance.

La Isla Shopping Village in Cancun combines new retailing opportunities for local residents with a wealth of entertainment opportunities for tourists.

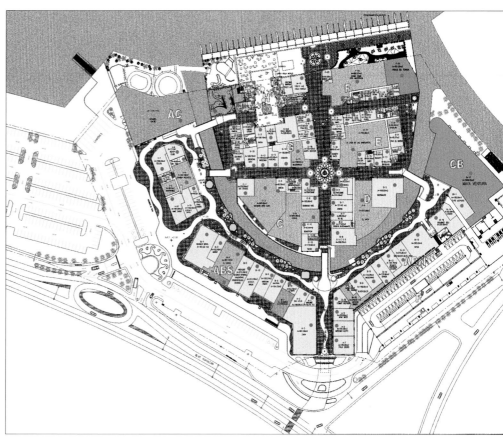

The site plan (above, right) shows the canal that was dredged to justify the "island" name. Caribbean architecture (right) contributes to the design theme.

Creating that ambiance, however, posed several challenges. The land did not allow the construction of a foundation for the structures, so 1,200 piles had to be placed underground to provide proper structural footing. So that the site could live up to its "island" name, an artificial water channel had to be dredged. The need to link the two principal commercial spaces, the Riverwalk and the island, offered design opportunities using bridges and handrails.

A tensile structure (above and near right) provides shade from the blazing Mexican sun. The Riverwalk (opposite) threads its way through La Isla, connecting to other parts of the center via bridges.

MAJOR TENANT		
NAME	**TYPE**	**GLA (SQ. FT.)**
Cinemark	Movie theaters	23,991
Interactive Aquarium	Aquarium	16,970
Zara	Apparel	15,728
La Casa de las Margaritas	Restaurant	7,604
Warner Bros. Studio Store	Apparel and entertainment retail	4,314

La Isla offers a rare treat: shoppers can arrive by boat at the center's own marina.

The ambience of a Mexican town comes across in storefront design.

Another major challenge was the much-needed protection from the sun and rain. The architect designed a tensile structure that would cover most of the common areas (the "streets"). Independent umbrella-like structures shelter visitors in the areas not shaded by the tensile structure. The various "streets" on the island each have themes and connect to a main avenue that runs from the main access to the marina at the west end of the project.

The center offers over 100 retailers. It created over 2,000 new jobs in addition to 3,500 indirect jobs. Many retailers on La Isla are new to Cancun, and the Warner Bros. Studio Store is the first in Latin America.

Waterfront promenades emphasize the center's island setting.

A six-level parking structure accommodates motorists. It connects to the shopping plaza through a mezzanine, which also serves as the cinema vestibule.

La Isla, recognized as one of the year's most innovative shopping centers in Mexico, has attracted widespread attention. Its design has been highlighted in architectural magazines. La Isla is proving to be a major draw for tourists visiting Cancun and a significant benefit to residents seeking employment and new retailers.

Small-pane windows reinforce the Caribbean architectural style that distinguishes La Isla.

Owner:

Ben Carter Properties
Atlanta, Georgia, United States

Simon Property Group
Indianapolis, Indiana, United States

Management Company:

Simon Property Group
Indianapolis, Indiana, United States

Architect/Designer:

TVS/Thompson Ventulett Stainback & Associates
Atlanta, Georgia, United States

Designer:

Communication Arts Inc./TVS
Boulder, Colorado/Atlanta, Georgia, United States

General Contractor:

Hardin Construction Group, Inc.
Atlanta, Georgia, United States

The Mall of Georgia at Mill Creek
Buford, Georgia, United States

Gross size of center:
1,793,413 sq. ft.

Gross leasable area excluding anchors:
908,413 sq. ft.

Total acreage of site:
120 acres

Type of center:
Super-regional center

Physical description:
Open and enclosed mall

Location of trading area:
Suburban

Population:
- Primary trading area
  521,216

- Secondary trading area
  192,233

- Annualized percentage of shoppers anticipated to be from outside trade area
  24%

Development schedule:
- Original opening date
  August 13, 1999

- Future expansion
  2002

Parking spaces:
- Present number
  8,384

- 1,000 parking spaces to be added

An aerial view of the Mall of Georgia shows how the curved enclosed mall surrounds the outdoor area.

Moviegoers can see past a dramatic fountain to the entry to the 20-screen cinema and IMAX theater.

Below, signs, towers and the village bandshell pay architectural homage to the regional styles of Georgia.

Photo: Don Johnson

*T*he Mall of Georgia at Mill Creek is the centerpiece of a 500-acre planned mixed-use community. The mall itself spans over 100 acres and includes a 20-screen movie theater, an IMAX 3-D cinema and a 700-seat food court. Much of the retail area is enclosed, but there is also an outdoor village.

The mall has many community amenities and focuses shoppers' attention on the history and culture of Georgia. Five distinctly themed courts represent the state's five geographic regions: Coastal, Plains, Atlanta, Piedmont and Mountain. In each court, memorabilia are on display, along with dramatic murals depicting regional life and information panels on each area's history.

Education also plays a role at the 80-acre nature park next to the outdoor village. In addition to offering a place for outdoor strolls, the trails in the nature park feature informational boards about the vegetation and habitats of Georgia.

The hometown feel of the Mall of Georgia extends to street signs and lampposts.

The outdoor areas (left and below) are rich in references to the small towns of Georgia.

The architect and designer found over 25 ways to unite the indoor and outdoor sections of the Mall of Georgia.

MAJOR TENANTS

NAME	TYPE	GLA (SQ. FT.)
Dillard's	Department store	240,000
Rich's	Department store	220,000
Nordstrom	Department store	160,000
JC Penney	Department store	145,000
Lord & Taylor	Apparel	120,000
Regal Cinemas	Multi-screen theater	115,000
Gaylan's	Sporting goods store	84,000
Bed Bath & Beyond	Housewares	42,000
Havertys	Furniture	42,000

Natural light, a large train shed volume and landscape create an attractive food court.

The architect and designer solved their initial challenge to blend the indoor and outdoor areas into a cohesive shopping experience: The master plan and lease plan created over 25 opportunities to visually and/or physically link the indoor and outdoor retail spaces. Extensive indoor landscaping also helps make the connection.

Ties to the community were the foundation of other development and design decisions as well. The immediate surroundings of the 500-acre master-planned Mill Creek mandated sensitivity to the area. Residents were encouraged to voice their opinions. The conservation aspects of the mall's plan, along with the outdoor retail space, won over the opposition of environmentalists, some homeowners and county officials. Even use of access roads built ties to the community, because there are two major accesses to the mall and no back entrance.

A clockface and stair railings harken back to earlier times of a train depot.

Successfully blending indoor and outdoor retailing is a significant step. The developer expects that this "one-stop" approach will characterize shopping center development in the 21st century by providing retailing, food, entertainment and nature on the same visit.

This court focuses on the Piedmont region of Georgia using a mural and educational panels.

Photos: Brian Gassel/TVS

Certificate of Merit

Owner:

Chelsea Property Group
Roseland, New Jersey, United States

Simon Property Group
Indianapolis, Indiana, United States

Architect/Designer:

Adams Hennon Architecture, PA
Mooresville, North Carolina, United States

General Contractor:

Hardin Construction Group, Inc.
Atlanta, Georgia, United States

Orlando Premium Outlets

Orlando, Florida, United States

Gross size of center:
473,992 sq. ft.

Gross leasable area excluding anchors:
429,365 sq. ft.

Total acreage of site:
46.04 acres

Type of center:
Outlet center

Physical description:
Partially covered center

Location of trading area:
Urban but not downtown

Population:
- Primary trading area
  3,151,900

- Secondary trading area
  6,362,200

- Annualized percentage of shoppers
  anticipated to be from outside trade area
  75%

Development schedule:
- Original opening date
  May 19, 2000

Parking spaces:
- Present number
  2,432

Photo: Smith Aerial

*T*he biggest design challenge facing Orlando Premium Outlets in Florida was visibility, from several very different vantage points. The site is located a great distance from an interstate, closer to a secondary road, and is also accessible to pedestrians. The designer addressed the issue by incorporating 100-foot-tall towers, massive hipped-roof structures and large screen walls for the interstate approach, while keeping to a smaller scale in other sections.

An aerial photograph of Orlando Premium Outlets shows its racetrack layout and partially covered walkways.

*Towers 100 feet tall
beckon motorists
from the distant
interstate highway.*

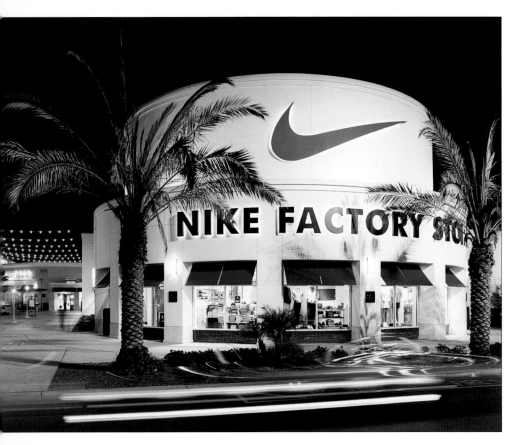

With the exception of one anchor store, the architectural design of the center recalls the South Florida Mediterranean style of the early 1900s, albeit interpreted by the vocabulary of the 1990s. The designer attributes the center's visual success to its design unity. Both developer and designer wanted to avoid thinly clad themed architecture and instead chose to take the classical Mediterranean idiom and design the center as though the style had continued to evolve over the past 80 years. This approach also allowed the buildings to work smoothly with such modern, straightforward elements as all-steel paseo roofs, glass curtain walls at each end of the food court, updated graphics and today's construction materials and methods.

MAJOR TENANTS		
NAME	**TYPE**	**GLA (SQ. FT.)**
Nike	Athletic fashion	19,318
Polo	Fashion	12,000
Banana Republic	Fashion	10,328
Reebok	Athletic fashion	9,907
Tommy Hilfiger	Fashion	9,192

Entryways to Orlando Premium Outlets (opposite) capitalize on the design identity of central Florida.

At least two important environmental issues were addressed through design. The hot and humid central Florida climate was successfully mitigated through the use of freestanding, naturally venting, shade-producing paseo roofs. The building also fits in well with existing neighbors and, says the designer, has a calming influence on its greater environment: the area surrounding Disney World.

Lampposts and benches offer street-like accents to the passageways between stores.

Covered walkways (above, left) provide needed shade from the Florida sun. Towering palms (left) bring Florida's outdoors inside, to the food court.

The mall is laid out in racetrack fashion, with covered walkways alternating with open areas. Color relies heavily on the coral, light pink and white palette found throughout Florida. Extensive landscaping features Florida palms. A wide variety of rooflines and fountains further enhance the ambience of Orlando Premium Outlets.

Contrasts in light and shade, indoors and out, offer a unique visual experience at Orlando Premium Outlets.

Photos: Mitchell Kearney Photography

Owner and Management Company:
Lincoln Harris/Pappas Properties/Post Properties
Charlotte, North Carolina, United States

Architect/Designer:
LS3P ASSOCIATES LTD.
Charlotte, North Carolina, United States

General Contractor:
Shelco
Charlotte, North Carolina, United States

Phillips Place
Charlotte, North Carolina, United States

Gross size of center:
130,000 sq. ft.

Gross leasable area excluding anchors:
130,000 sq. ft.

Total acreage of site:
35 acres

Type of center:
Regional center

Physical description:
Open mall

Location of trading area:
Suburban

Population:
• Primary trading area
 1,200,000

Development schedule:
• Original opening dates
 1997-00

Parking spaces:
• Present number
 1,412

Phillips Place is a 35-acre site whose major components are 100,000 square feet of retail and restaurants, a 10-screen cinema, a 123-suite hotel and 430 multi-family residential units. The vision for Phillips Place was to integrate these components into a pedestrian-friendly environment organized around an interior "main street" with two-way automotive traffic and angle parking on each side.

What at first glance resembles a quiet downtown scene is part of the mixed-use Phillips Place (left). An all-suites hotel (above) anchors the western end of the project. Retail occupies the center of the site, as shown on the site plan (below).

LEGEND

☐ RETAIL
▨ MIXED USE
☐ THEATRE
☐ HOTEL
▨ MULTI-FAMILY

Brick streets and sidewalks, old-style roof moldings and abundant landscaping make it look as though Phillips Place has been there for decades.

The north side of the street contains retail and entertainment spaces designed to accommodate second-level mezzanine space. The south side consists of three-story buildings comprised of ground-level retail and multi-family housing in a mixture of two-story townhouses and flats. The theater anchors the eastern terminus, and the six-story hotel anchors the west. A central square, for outdoor entertainment and dining, is visible from the balconies of upper-story apartments. Parking at the site is distributed around the perimeters of buildings; the site's natural slope allowed for two-level, tray-type decks, providing abundant parking near the theaters.

As picturesque as a movie set, the main street has become a popular gathering place.

MAJOR TENANTS

NAME	TYPE	GLA (SQ. FT.)
Palm Steakhouse	Restaurant	6,900
Upstream	Restaurant	7,000
Dean & Deluca	Food emporium	7,500
Phillips Place Cinemas	Theater	30,000
Smith & Hawken	Gardening	5,007
Coplon's	Apparel	7,500
Restoration Hardware	Home furnishings	8,850
Waverly Home	Home furnishings	5,511
P.F. Chang's China Bistro	Restaurant	6,824

The only modern-looking features at the multiplex cinema are the movies themselves.

Shoppers' focus on "main street" and its design presented a few unforeseen challenges. For example, parking decks — deliberately well disguised by typography and landscape — were not obvious to first-time shoppers.

Buildings feature a classical palette of light earth tones, creating a visual cohesion for the project. Different coloration of the synthetic stucco of the wall surfaces allows a range of hues within the general order provided by the architecture. Complementary-colored canvas awnings further contribute to the visual variety.

Head-in and angle parking (above, left) reinforce the downtown look of Phillips Place. Signage (above, right) matches the design concept. Open space (below) is abundant, adding to the community feeling of Phillips Place.

Built on the largest undeveloped tract in the SouthPark area of Charlotte, the project was the first mixed-use center built in the city in 40 years. As a result, there were intense negotiations with the city zoning department to allow this special use. Residents' original objection to more retail in their community was overcome by the innovative mix of uses and active streetscape that the project provided.

Many indicators evidence the project's success. Rents at the Phillips Place apartments are the highest in the city, and the center's restaurants are the busiest. The developer reports that other projects are being launched nationally, using the concepts tested at Phillips Place.

Residential units occupy space above some retail areas.

Fountains and building edifices hark back to a bygone era, but they remain distinguishing features of the new Phillips Place.

Photos: R. Alexander & Associates

Certificate of Merit

Owner:
Providence Place Group, L. P.
Providence, Rhode Island, United States

Management Company:
Commonwealth Development Group
Providence, Rhode Island, United States

Architect:
Arrowstreet Inc.
Somerville, Massachusetts, United States

Designer:
Frederich St. Florian
Providence, Rhode Island, United States

General Contractor:
Morse Diesel International
Boston, Massachusetts, United States

Providence Place
Providence, Rhode Island, United States

Gross size of center:
3.5 million sq. ft.

Gross leasable area excluding anchors:
731,000 sq. ft.

Total acreage of site:
13.2 acres

Type of center:
Super-regional center

Physical description:
Enclosed multi-level mall

Location of trading area:
Urban/suburban

Population:
• Primary trading area
1,000,000

• Secondary trading area
1,200,000

• Annualized percentage of shoppers
anticipated to be from outside trade area
20%

Development schedule:
• Original opening date
August 20, 1999

Parking spaces:
• Present number
4,500

Abundant natural light and large cutout areas open up the interior of Providence Place. The Wintergarden's glass wall is clearly visible from the River Walk (below).

*P*rovidence Place is a key component of the revitalization of a 60-acre section of downtown Providence, Rhode Island, adjacent to the historic state capitol. Revitalization plans for the area had been implemented in phases over the past eight years and included building new roads, reopening rivers that had been enclosed in conduits and creating public park space and walking corridors. A skybridge links Providence Place to the convention center and a hotel. Adjacent to a new River Walk and the state capitol, Providence Place also benefits from having one of the nation's most-traveled interstates as its western border. The center bridges the Amtrak northeast rail corridor, one of the most heavily used in the U.S.

The 11-story parking and retail complex fully integrates into Providence's Federal-style architecture, complementing the state capitol. The brick facade, with its large punched windows and extensive glazing, echoes many historic industrial buildings.

Providence Place brought retail back to downtown by revitalizing under-used riverfront property that had great potential.

The major design challenge was to span 160 feet across the railroad tracks and the river. This was achieved with a three-story glazed Wintergarden. The transparency of the Wintergarden windows reduces the perceived mass of the building and projects light and activity out to the city. The structure crossing the river is wide enough to house shops and the food court. This structural

Pedestrian bridges (above) link the project to other downtown facilities.

Pedestrian traffic flow between mall levels (left) is encouraged by clear views from lower to upper floors. The presence of Providence Place has given new life (above) to eateries on surrounding streets, where diners enjoy views of the state capitol.

MAJOR TENANTS		
NAME	**TYPE**	**GLA (SQ. FT.)**
Filene's	Department store	204,000
Nordstrom	Department store	195,000
Hoyts Cinema 16	Multi-screen theaters	114,589
Lord & Taylor	Department store	120,000
Feinstein IMAX	Theater	13,557

solution required caissons eight feet in diameter and 22-foot-deep trusses each installed in two pieces over active rail lines.

The 26,000 tons of structural steel used in the project overall was the largest steel order in the U.S. in 1998.

Although Providence had been growing dramatically in recent years, it did not have a critical mass of retail and entertainment options. Providence Place satisfies that need. The rooftop contains an IMAX theatre and a multiplex cinema as well as other entertainment venues. These facilities necessitate accommodating visitors after-hours through the parking, food court and mall areas.

The Providence Place interior clearly points to Nordstrom, one of the center's anchors.

Photo: Peter Goldberg

Natural light flows into the multi-level mall area. The food court (right) benefits from the large glass wall of the Wintergarden.

An aerial view of Providence Place shows how the Wintergarden spans the Woonasquatucket River.

The mall also created an active street level between downtown and the state capitol. The main street between the two is now lined primarily with restaurants and other retail locations. The River Walk was extended from original plans to link to downtown as well. In addition, Providence Place gave the city an opportunity to present a good "face" to the passing interstate, which is apparent in the attention to design along the back side of the project.

Providence's rebirth and the success of Providence Place have drawn the attention of national media and four other developers, who shortly thereafter announced plans to build over 700 luxury residential units, 125,000 more square feet of retail space and over 300,000 square feet of office space.

Certificate of Merit

Owner:

RPS II L.L.C.
Spokane, Washington, United States

Management Company:

R. W. Robideaux & Company
Spokane, Washington, United States

Architect/Designer:

Callison Architecture, Inc.
Seattle, Washington, United States

General Contractor:

Robert Goebel General Contractors
Spokane, Washington, United States

River Park Square
Spokane, Washington, United States

Gross size of center:
533,000 sq. ft.

Gross leasable area excluding anchors:
180,000 sq. ft.

Total acreage of site:
2.8 acres

Type of center:
Fashion/specialty center

Physical description:
Enclosed mall

Location of trading area:
Urban central business district

Population:
- Primary trading area
  500,000

- Secondary trading area
  1,700,000

Development schedule:
- Original opening date
  August 1999

Parking spaces:
- Present number
  750

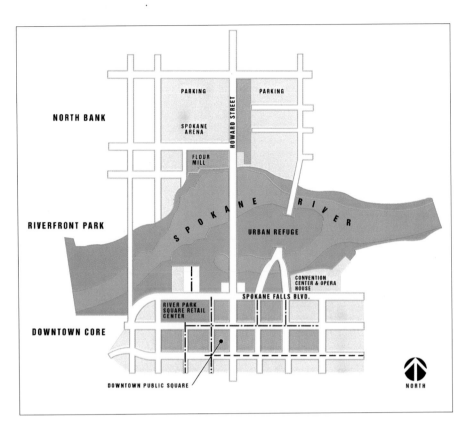

R iver Park Square is the cornerstone of a community-wide effort to expand the downtown Spokane retail, entertainment and visitor district. It covers two blocks within a several-block neighborhood of smaller-scaled distinguished buildings three and four stories tall. The mall is located across the street from the popular Riverfront Park.

River Park Square is part of Spokane's downtown core and directly adjacent to the popular River Front Park (above). Exterior design of the mall (left) kept the brick and steel facade, window shapes and height consistent with surrounding buildings. Festive lighting (opposite) shines through the atrium at street level.

By respecting the scale, materials and nearby historic buildings, the brick and steel River Park Square appears to be part of a collection of buildings that grew into inviting neighborhood blocks over time. Varied forms, staggered building heights, arched windows, individual storefronts and window openings reinforce this sense of unity while giving tenants the opportunity to express their own identities.

At the heart of River Park Square is a 100-foot-tall glass atrium that serves as an enclosed plaza and a showcase for regionally inspired artworks. Illuminated at night, the atrium becomes a beacon for downtown shopping and entertainment.

A map showing northwestern lakes dominates one entryway to the mall and builds ties to the community.

The atrium (below) towers three floors high and is surrounded by the multiplex cinema on the fourth and fifth levels (below, left).

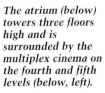

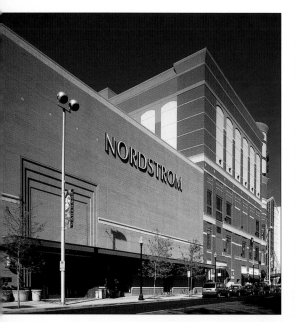

Retailers have made a strong presence at street level through signage.

The steel and brick design concept (below) unites interior and exterior. Jutting balconies (right) vary sight lines at the upper levels of the mall.

The tight urban site — only 2.8 acres — presented major challenges. A level of underground parking had to be added. Utilities that were 100 years old had to be moved or upgraded. The soon-to-be-relocated Nordstrom and existing parking had to be kept open throughout construction. Also, the construction staging area was extremely small, forcing the construction company to maneuver equipment and supplies in and out of the project while occupying just a single traffic lane.

MAJOR TENANTS		
NAME	**TYPE**	**GLA (SQ. FT.)**
Nordstrom	Department store	130,000
AMC Theaters	Multi-screen theater	90,000

River Park Square addressed a problem common among cities, the specter of department stores relocating to the suburbs. River Park Square, however, offered a vital alternative by reviving downtown Spokane and bringing in new daytime and nighttime traffic. Indeed, the project attracted new retailers to the region that may not have considered downtown locations or this market before.

The project benefits the city's use of land – although River Park Square required the vacating of one city street, it has enhanced the pedestrian connection to River Front Park. Since the mall's opening, over $200 million worth of additional building investment has taken place in its vicinity.

River Park Square has revitalized downtown Spokane, bringing in more shoppers by day and night.

Certificate of Merit

Owner and Management Company:
General Growth Properties, Inc. – Grandville L.L.C.
Chicago, Illinois, United States

Architect/Designer:
KA, Inc. Architecture
Cleveland, Ohio, United States

General Contractor:
Taylor-Ball
Des Moines, Iowa, United States

RiverTown Crossings
Grandville, Michigan, United States

Gross size of center:
1,290,000 sq. ft.

Gross leasable area excluding anchors:
413,090 sq. ft.

Total acreage of site:
138 acres

Type of center:
Super-regional center

Physical description:
Enclosed mall

Location of trading area:
Suburban

Population:
- Primary trading area
  800,000

- Secondary trading area
  1,200,000

- Annualized percentage of shoppers
  anticipated to be from outside trade area
  20%

Development schedule:
- Original opening date
  November 3, 1999

Parking spaces:
- Present number
  6,408

RiverTown Crossings, a two-level enclosed mall, is designed as a place for families to shop and be entertained. Centrally located in western Michigan, it has five department stores, a sports anchor, a multi-screen cinema, a 1,000-seat food court and 113 specialty stores and restaurants.

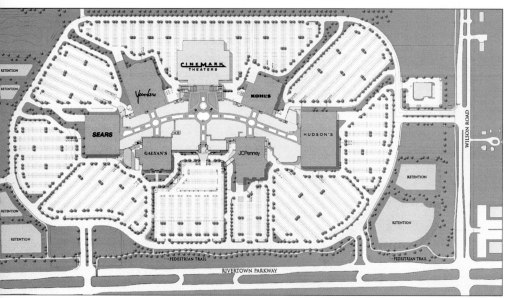

The massive nature of the RiverTown Crossings project (aerial view and site map, above) brought objections from local activists, who were later won over by the community and family aspects of the mall.

Star-studded visual design and nautical references abound at RiverTown Crossings.

Development necessitated a number of major undertakings, including new and improved access roads, an abundance of directional signage and the relocation of an existing stream and wetlands. The cool, damp Michigan climate prompted the building of covered parking at both front and rear lots. Bicycle and walking trails surround the mall and connect to the local high school.

Some leasing aspects had development solutions, particularly the need to keep "big box" users (restaurants and bookstores in particular) from looking elsewhere. The developers chose to position these tenants on the front of the mall, in optimum locations between department stores and adjacent to the main mall entrance. Escalators and stairs are placed so as not to obstruct views of small stores or anchors.

Murals and glazed graphics (left and above) make references to the culture of western Michigan. The designer took every opportunity to add light and reflections to offset the cloudy Michigan climate (right).

Family lounges provide "time-out" opportunities for shoppers who need a break.

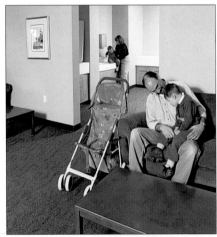

Plantings and open space (left) surround the guest services area. Carpets and soft seating groupings (above) are found in six locations throughout the center.

Lighting plays an important role, given Michigan's propensity for limited sunlight. Glazing was integrated into the building architecture in many forms, such as skylights, dormers and clerestories, to provide natural light whenever possible. All glazing has frittered patterns to pick up reflections at night so the glass does not go black. Both functional and decorative lighting, including colored neon, provide a bright and festive mood at night.

The family aspect of RiverTown Crossings inspired restrooms on two levels, including large family lounges, changing areas, family toilets with child-sized fixtures and facilities for the handicapped and senior citizens. An extra-high carousel was installed, as well as carpeted soft seating areas in six locations throughout the mall. A local hospital subsidized a children's play area.

MAJOR TENANTS

NAME	TYPE	GLA (SQ. FT.)
Hudson's	Department store	165,754
Younkers	Department store	150,081
Sears	Department store	124,245
JC Penney	Department store	105,780
Galyan's	Sporting goods	91,348
Kohl's	Department store	89,048
Cinemark	Multi-screen theater	86,410

A local hospital donated this children's playground to the mall and its family customers.

To emphasize the community aspect of the mall, an artist was commissioned to paint seven large murals depicting western Michigan themes – one of which stretches 330 feet. The food court features Michigan lighthouses on its tabletops and nautical flags in the floor paving. A "School Spirit" retail space features memorabilia and activities from three local high schools. This store also provides local high school students with retail training.

Initial local reaction to such a large project was mixed, but the family and community aspects of the mall have persuaded opposing groups that the center is a benefit to the area. RiverTown Crossings has since become a major attraction of the western Michigan market.

A carousel is just one of the many family-focused attractions at RiverTown Crossings.

Owner:
GGP Ala Moana L.L.C.
Honolulu, Hawaii, United States

Management Company:
General Growth Management of Hawaii, Inc.
Honolulu, Hawaii, United States

Architect:
DLR Group
Seattle, Washington, United States

Anbe Aruga and Ishizu
Honolulu, Hawaii, United States

Designer:
Callison Architecture, Inc.
Seattle, Washington, United States

General Contracor:
Fletcher Pacific Construction Co.; Hawaii Dredging Construction Co.
Honolulu, Hawaii, United States

Ala Moana Center
Honolulu, Hawaii, United States

Gross size of center:
1,800,000 sq. ft.

Amount of space added or renovated:
300,000 sq. ft.

Gross leasable area excluding anchors:
910,000 sq. ft.

Total acreage of site:
50 acres

Type of center:
Super-regional center

Physical description:
Open mall

Location of trading area:
Urban but not downtown

Population:
- Primary trading area:
  512,400
- Secondary trading area:
  664,789
- Annualized percentage of shoppers anticipated to be from outside trade area 40%

Development schedule:
- Original opening date
  September 1959
- Current expansion date
  Spring 1999

Parking spaces
- Present number
  8,502
- 478 parking spaces added in renovation

The renovation at Ala Moana Center changed the undistinguished Liberty House facade (above) into Hawaiian-influenced design (opposite).

The owner recognized the capacity of the 40-year-old Ala Moana Center to draw almost every visitor, tourist and local resident – if the shopping experience could be repositioned to appeal to each type of customer. The renovation began simultaneously with a significant shift in shopping patterns, resulting primarily from a slowdown in the Japanese economy. Since the center had a strong orientation toward that particular customer, it was decided that the renovation gave Ala Moana the opportunity to reposition itself, away from the Asian tourist and toward the local customer, by providing a community destination and an urban amenity.

A row of potted palms accents subtly shaded edifices.

An old trellis roof (left) gave way to open sky (below) and a village concept.

Shots from before (above) and after (right) show how new design brought Ala Moana into the 21st century, Hawaiian style.

The renovation included adding a three-level Neiman Marcus and a center-wide third level with 140,000 square feet of leasable area. The food court would be enlarged and parking added. Unfortunately, the original structure was not designed for a vertical expansion; floor-to-floor heights were twice what they should have been for such a renovation, presenting both structural and aesthetic challenges.

Preparations for the vertical expansion required a three-year head start. The first task was to strengthen the columns on the two existing stories. This was done when tenants changed over, while the shops were vacant. In cases where tenant leases continued during the remodeling period, work was done at night.

Another construction challenge was the existing center's open-air areas, where shoppers could be vulnerable to falling construction debris from surrounding roofs. A temporary plywood cover was built to protect shoppers from work overhead. In the lower-level shops, unistructure systems were brought in for tenants to use for hanging their ceiling equipments while the old ceilings were torn out. Phase-in of a new parking deck took over two years, to allow for sufficient parking while some lots were being remodeled.

MAJOR TENANTS

NAME	TYPE	GLA (SQ. FT.)
Sears	Department store	341,199
Liberty House	Department store	326,860
JC Penney	Department store	182,351
Neiman Marcus	Department store	161,055

Renovation (opposite page, all) made the Hawaiian sunshine part of the visual beauty of the center. A new design approach was critical for the food court (above). Today, diners are surrounded by Hawaiian vistas: the sea and its colorful denizens (left).

Interior design sought to "de-mall" the center by creating an eclectic, village-style design of varying scales, forms and materials. Lighting, landscaping and architecture were carefully integrated to convey the spirit of Hawaii. Building upwards also allowed the developer to create a direct visual connection to the ocean and mountains.

The food court's location in a windowless space at a lower level presented another challenge. In expanding the food court to 1,100 seats, the designer decided to capitalize on the cultural roots and symbols of Hawaii, overlaying three-dimensional objects to create an imaginary world so that diners can forget they are in the lower level of a shopping center.

Ala Moana has now been dramatically repositioned for the next few decades, having been renewed through architecture, design and sensitivity to the community.

A fountain and small-scale stores underscore the village aspect of Ala Moana Center.

Owner:
Gandel Retail Trust and Gandel Group
Melbourne, Victoria, Australia

Management Company:
Gandel Management Limited
Melbourne, Victoria, Australia

Architect/Designer:
RTKL
Los Angeles, California, United States

The Buchan Group
Melbourne, Victoria, Australia

General Contractor:
Probuild
Melbourne, Victoria, Australia

Chadstone Shopping Centre
Melbourne, Victoria, Australia

Gross size of center:
1,326,000 sq. ft.

Amount of space added or renovated:
354,000 sq. ft.

Gross leasable area excluding anchors:
496,491 sq. ft.

Total acreage of site:
68 acres

Type of center:
Super-regional center

Physical description:
Enclosed mall

Location of trading area:
Suburban

Population:
• Primary trading area
342,000

• Secondary trading area
645,000

• Annualized percentage of shoppers anticipated to be from outside trade area
30%

Development schedule:
• Original opening date
November 1960

• Current expansion date
December 1999

• Future expansion
December 2000

Parking spaces:
• Present number
8,000

• 2,700 parking spaces added in renovation

*C*hadstone Shopping Centre, one of Australia's first regional malls, was built in 1960. Since then, its commitment to well-planned expansions and a strong fashion-oriented retail mix has kept it at the forefront of Australian retailing.

Chadstone Shopping Centre at night features dramatic lighting, sculpture and window displays. The curved glass atrium (opposite) defines the expansion.

A master plan developed in the early 1990s led to a renovation that opened its doors in December 1999, re-creating Chadstone with Australian and international designer boutiques, two new department stores, homewares stores and a new cinema complex. The expansion's focal point is a sweeping, curved glass roof that serves as a counterpoint to the classic linear galleria that shapes the rest of the center. The curved glass atrium ends in nautilus-shaped knuckles at the north and south ends. With no trusses or columns between the end courts, the atrium provides superior sight lines. It is also easily visible and identifiable from the highway.

Minimalist, classic design is used throughout. Along the highway, the landscape design features rustic bands of low groundcover grass and stone, allowing the building itself to take center stage. The paving in the nautilus courts is a concentric radial pattern of gold, red and black granite. The basket-weave pattern of the paving matches shadows cast by the sun streaming through the spiraled glass.

Storefronts (above and right) maintain a noteworthy presence without needing to compete with the undulating atrium overhead.

A sculptural feline watches over a busy outdoor eatery.

MAJOR TENANTS		
NAME	**TYPE**	**GLA (SQ. FT.)**
Myer	Department store	234,000
David Jones	Department store	179,880
Hoyts	Multi-screen theater	96,404
Target	Discount department store	92,174
Kmart	Discount department store	69,052
Coles	Supermarket	48,266
Bi-Lo	Supermarket	40,818
Toys 'Я' Us	Toys and apparel	31,657
AMF	Bowling alley	21,980

A dramatic water feature draws the eye upward toward other retail floors (right). Public art (above) fits in with the fashion focus of Chadstone.

Anchors are readily identified by strong signage.

All interior finishes have been kept minimalist as well: French limestone flooring, landscaping accented by bamboo plantings and antique or polished bronze on vertical and horizontal finishes. Artworks, including specially commissioned sculptures by Australian artists, add a dramatic effect inside and out and suit the fashion orientation of the mall. Two water sculptures and large public spaces with comfortable seating and washrooms further enhance the center.

Throughout the expansion, the architect and designers kept in touch with the surrounding community, seeking opinions. Traffic was a major concern; as a result, after-hours access is limited to the highway exits. To abate noise, the center built acoustic fences. Landscaping provides a green buffer near residential areas. During the construction, the developer made significant contributions to improving public parklands and sporting facilities nearby.

Clear and minimalist concepts extend even to store and transportation signage.

While the center's popularity makes the developer wish he had built even more eateries than the four already added, he credits project planning and market research for the success of the renovation and expansion of Chadstone Shopping Centre.

Details at a water feature and in floor coverings point to the close attention to design at Chadstone Shopping Centre.

Owner and Management Company:
Simon Property Group
Indianapolis, Indiana, United States

Architect/Designer:
Altoon + Porter Architects LLP
Los Angeles, California, United States

General Contractor:
DPMI
Mission Viejo, California, United States

The Shops at Mission Viejo
Mission Viejo, California, United States

Gross size of center:
1,162,503 sq. ft.

Amount of space added or renovated:
319,302 sq. ft.

Gross leasable area excluding anchors:
474,686 sq. ft.

Total acreage of site:
67 acres

Type of center:
Super-regional center

Physical description:
Enclosed two-level mall

Location of trading area:
Suburban

Population:
• Primary trading area
  521,325

• Annualized percentage of shoppers
  anticipated to be from outside trade area
  29%

Development schedule:
• Original opening date
  October 1979

• Current expansion date
  September 1999

Parking spaces:
• Present number
  5,905

• 1,959 parking spaces added in
  renovation

New signage (above, left and right) symbolizes the big changes from the old Mission Viejo Mall (above).

*T*he Shops at Mission Viejo is an expansion and refurbishment of the Mission Viejo Mall, an enclosed two-level mall that, according to the developer, "was dated when it was first built" in 1979. It faced extraordinarily strong competition from regional malls nearby. The low price-points of its retailers — who were mostly leasing on a month-to-month basis — did little to attract the increasingly affluent residents of south Orange County. Few national chains remained within the mall. Food was not consolidated and the outdated cinema did little to attract more visitors to the mall.

The lush land-scaping at The Shops at Mission Viejo includes rotating seasonal arrangements.

New, updated entryway styles (right) offer a much more inviting approach than the entrances in the former design (above).

A gently undulating balustrade and curved overhangs (right) update the interior of the mall from its previous reliance on right angles (above).

The strong competitive presence required the mall to have a different appeal from nearby centers, as well as a different look. The decision was made to remake the mall into "resort retail," evoking a sense of casual elegance, and re-name it The Shops at Mission Viejo.

The casual elegance sought in the renovation is reflected in the entries to the Saks anchor, the food court, at the Nordstrom court and in the mall area (opposite page).

The most important task for the mall was to reconnect with its primary trade area shoppers, to encourage them to return to the mall as their first choice for shopping. To achieve this, an old Montgomery Ward store was transformed into two levels of inline shops. A new two-level Nordstrom store was built on the Ward's old parking lot. A new two-level Saks Fifth Avenue signified upper-end retailing and also attracted upper-end small stores. The smaller of two existing Robinson's-May stores was remodeled into specialty destinations. A large food court was added.

To reinforce the "resort retail" image, 68 new skylights were cut into the roof and ceiling, bringing an abundance of daylight into the center. Formal and random stone floor patterns using Bavarian limestone and marble imbued the mall with an upscale look. The ceiling system, flooring, storefront surrounds and handrails were re-designed. Curves and brushed stainless railings were added to bridges that cross over the mall on the second level. Hues inside the mall, while brighter than colors in the previous design, are muted to give the storefronts center stage. Vertical circulation was relocated and replaced. A new central court fountain draws crowds at all hours.

MAJOR TENANTS		
NAME	**TYPE**	**GLA (SQ. FT.)**
Robinson's	Department store	224,315
Macy's	Department store	202,785
Nordstrom	Department store	160,000
Saks Fifth Avenue	Department store	100,000
Old Navy	Clothing	41,466

A pineapple — the symbol of hospitality — welcomes patrons at the food court.

Lighting design was a major element to communicate the "resort retail" ambience of the renovated mall.

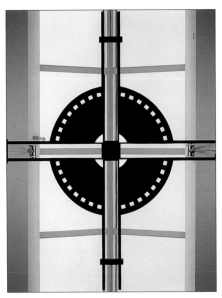

The soft and refined glow from light fixtures — reminiscent of hotel lobbies — allows tenant storefronts to be brighter at The Shops at Mission Viejo.

Even the decision to eliminate the small outdated cinema strengthened the mall's image of casual elegance; the absence of groups of teenagers drawn by the movie theater has encouraged adult shoppers to stay longer. The synergy of these many decisions rejuvenated the mall, placing The Shops at Mission Viejo back among the top competitors in the market.

Owner:

Alabang Commercial Corporation
Muntinlupa City, Philippines

Management Company:

Ayala Land, Inc.
Makati City, Philippines

Architect:

Architecture International
Mill Valley, California, United States

GF and Partners, Architects Co.
Makati City, Philippines

Designer:

RMDA Architects
Makati City, Philippines

Robert A. Alejandro
Quezon City, Philippines

General Contractor:

Gammon Philippines, Inc.
Makati City, Philippines

Alabang Town Center
Muntinlupa City, Philippines

Gross size of center:
916,015 sq. ft.

Amount of space added or renovated:
319,580 sq. ft.

Gross leasable area excluding anchors:
503,780 sq. ft.

Total acreage of site:
43.24 acres

Type of center:
Regional center

Physical description:
Hybrid mall

Location of trading area:
Suburban

Population:
* Primary trading area
  1,288,650
* Secondary trading area
  1,880,615
* Annualized percentage of shoppers
  anticipated to be from outside trade area
  10%

Development schedule:
* Original opening date
  June 1982
* Current expansion date
  July 1997

Parking spaces:
* Present number
  2,690
* 1,680 parking spaces added in expansion

Alabang Town Center (ATC) started in 1982 as a strip mall containing a supermarket and two cinemas. As the surrounding area grew, the developers commissioned a master plan to unify the undistinguished compound of structures into a true community center. Soon thereafter, four regional shopping centers opened with a combined leasable area of 5.8 million square feet. While ATC was far from deteriorating, and had never experienced vacancies nor significant drops in sales, the developers realized that its small size and limited tenant mix would jeopardize the center's market share. The developers chose to recreate the Town Center as a lifestyle center.

An aerial view (above, right) shows Alabang Town Center in the foreground. An interior court (below left) is dotted with stars and suns overhead. The Town Plaza (right) includes a low gilded fountain, an amphitheater and a stage.

Skylights (left and right) shed soft illumination in a store and a mall walkway. Corte de las Palmas (below) is the major entrance to Alabang Town Center.

A playground (left), eateries (below) and a mall area (right) demonstrate how Alabang Town Center serves the local community.

The goals of the renovation were to: reposition ATC as a regional retail/entertainment center without losing its town appeal; develop nighttime destination potential; increase retail space by 100 percent with 200 new shops and a department store; and maintain the relaxed atmosphere for which ATC had become known – in addition to improving sales, broadening merchandising categories and price points, and increasing traffic flow.

Adding nearly 320,000 square feet of leasable area achieved those goals. The space is designed around a five-story atrium, which also serves as a community activity center. An amusement center and electronics and appliance stores are on the third story.

MAJOR TENANTS		
NAME	**TYPE**	**GLA (SQ. FT.)**
Rustan's	Department store	85,179
Makati Supermarket	Supermarket	81,333
South Supermarket	Supermarket	75,911
True Value	Hardware	23,299
Cinderella	Department store	16,194
Tower Records	Music store	8,241

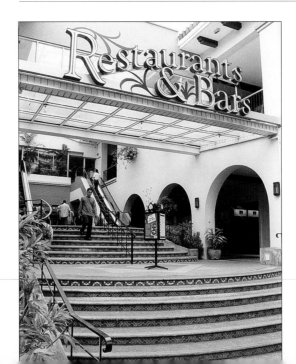

The center's major entrance, the Corte de las Palmas, is filled with color, texture and sound. Overhead it is dominated by an open web vault, supported by six telescoping steel masts rising more than two stories and topped by alternating translucent and opaque bands of roofing.

The phased-in building plan, constrained by existing structures, was complicated. A continuous information and marketing campaign was in place during renovation and expansion. Bulletins informed nearby villages of the progress of work and what to expect. Specially posted security guards rerouted

Filipino architecture, landscaping and steel cutout icons pay tribute to the cultural heritage of the community.

At right, palms and water displays create an attractive ambience for community gathering.

*A playground helps
Alabang Town
Center live up to its
name.*

pedestrian and vehicular traffic away from construction. Mall-wide sales helped sustain shoppers' interest. An art contest allowed children to paint the board-ups that surrounded construction areas. Only marginal drops in sales and traffic occurred.

In the expanded and renovated center, local artists were commissioned to design distinctive imagery with a Filipino twist. Icons of everyday life, including the horse-drawn carriage, jeeps, the marketplace, street vendors and tributes to national flora and fauna, add local flavor to the center.

The tenant mix was also vastly improved, with best-selling international merchants brought in — many opening their only store in the Philippines. Together with the entertainment and food components, the tenant mix has revitalized Alabang Town Center into a community center as well.

Certificate of Merit

Owner and Management Company:
Simon Property Group
Indianapolis, Indiana, United States

Architect/Designer:
TVS/Thompson Ventulett Stainback & Associates
Atlanta, Georgia, United States

General Contractor:
DeBartolo Property Management
Youngstown, Ohio, United States

The Florida Mall
Orlando, Florida, United States

Gross size of center:
1,633,055 sq. ft.

Amount of space added or renovated:
414,690 sq. ft.

Gross leasable area excluding anchors:
584,901 sq. ft.

Total acreage of site:
144.1 acres

Type of center:
Super-regional center

Physical description:
Enclosed mall

Location of trading area:
Suburban

Population:
- Primary trading area
  300,543
- Secondary trading area
  201,110
- Annualized percentage of shoppers anticipated to be from outside trade area
  35%

Development schedule:
- Original opening date
  November 1988
- Current expansion date
  November 1999
- Future expansion
  October 2002

Parking spaces:
- Present number
  3,642

An aerial view of The Florida Mall shows the expansion area on the left side of the photograph. The old mall entrance (above, left) was nondescript.

The new entry (above) boldly states its case. An old court is cluttered and offers no sense of identity (below, left). Graphics overhead unify the updated version (below, right).

*F*lorida Mall looked dated. Built in the late 1980s as a super-regional mall with five department store anchors and still dominant in its Orlando market, the mall's developer decided that it was time for renovation and expansion. Resident population growth and increasing diversity of the tourist market merited a new design approach. The original design had a disjointed collection of dated themes: Mediterranean, Art Deco and Victorian Main Street. Existing courts were rambling spaces without any sense of place or definition. The merchandise mix was limited and not representative of the potential customer base.

Continuous skylighting (above) pulls customers through the turns of the racetrack layout in the expanded mall. Interior "windows" give a smaller sense of scale within the large mall (below).

The expansion and new design sought to give The Florida Mall an identity in keeping with the demographics of its customers, both local and tourist. The addition of a new Burdines department store and the consolidation of two Dillard's locations offered the impetus for an expansion wing developed in racetrack layout. Each leg of the racetrack passes through an "oasis" court — a welcome seating area at its midpoint — before joining together in a curved skylit concourse linking the Burdines court with two new entrances.

Expansion of the mall created the extra lease area for stores that would help achieve the range of price points that would enable The Florida Mall to address its varied customer base. Higher price-point merchandising — missing in the old mall — could now be accommodated. Architectural treatments and decor also addressed this issue.

MAJOR TENANTS		
NAME	**TYPE**	**GLA (SQ. FT.)**
Dillard's	Department store	252,300
JC Penney	Department store	200,000
Budines	Department store	200,000
Sears	Department store	169,926
Parisian	Department store	120,256
Saks Fifth Avenue	Department store	105,672

Arched portals with louvered transoms define smaller rooms within the racetrack concourse.

Paler floor patterns (above) are more generous to store displays and signage than the earlier design (below).

*Food court tabletops
incorporate Florida
plant and animal life
into their patterns.
The food court (right
and opposite) benefits
from natural light
from above.*

The new racetrack wing also
offered the opportunity for some
specialized leasing. The leg
connecting Saks to Burdines was
merchandised with an upscale
mix of lifestyle tenants that were
not then in the Orlando market.
The leg from Burdines to Dillard's
focused on tenants that cater to
children, teenagers and "twenty-
somethings" of the more affluent
community.

The renovation was given the
same dramatic architectural
language as the expansion,
eliminating the disjointed themes
of the old mall. Smaller, more
intimate spaces were created
inside the vast volumes that had
previously characterized the
existing court areas.

In the renovated area, over 40
tenants were re-merchandised to
better serve the customers seeking
middle and lower price points. A
new entrance pavilion serves as
both a glowing beacon and a
memorable icon for the renovated
mall.

Striking storefronts at a toy store reflect the entertainment focus of the market served by The Florida Mall.

Overall, the expansion and renovation of The Florida Mall show how an already successful mall can evolve to meet the needs of its changing customer base.

Owner:
Metropolitan Airports Commission
Minneapolis, Minnesota, United States

Management Company:
Host Marriott
St. Paul, Minnesota, United States

Architect:
Architectural Alliance
Minneapolis, Minnesota, United States

Designer:
Dennis LaFrance & David Thorpe
Minneapolis, Minnesota, United States

General Contractor:
Morcon General Contractors
Golden Valley, Minnesota, United States

Northstar Crossing at Minneapolis/St. Paul International Airport
St. Paul, Minnesota, United States

Gross size of center:
120,000 sq. ft.

Amount of space added or renovated:
16,000 sq. ft. added,
72,000 sq. ft. renovated

Gross leasable area excluding anchors:
72,000 sq. ft.

Total acreage of site:
3,100 acres

Type of center:
Community center

Physical description:
Enclosed mall

Location of trading area:
Airport

Population:
- Primary trading area
  80,000
- Secondary trading area
  1,000,000
- Annualized percentage of shoppers anticipated to be from outside trade area
  45%

Development schedule:
- Original opening date
  July 1968
- Current expansion date
  December 1999
- Future expansion
  January 2003

Parking spaces:
- Present number
  13,302

Northstar Crossing is a redevelopment of the food, beverage and merchandise retailers at the Minneapolis-St. Paul International Airport. The airport, built in the mid-1960s, placed concessions in the crossroads between airline concourses. Until recently, concessions and retail shops were given low priority in the operation of the airport. Coffee shops and newsstands were inefficiently squeezed into available concourse openings without an overall plan.

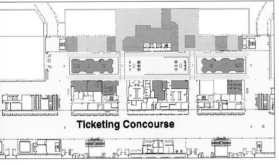

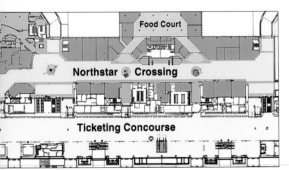

Northstar Crossing at the Minneapolis/ St. Paul International Airport is located behind and adjacent to the ticketing concourse.

Passengers shop, eat and browse during layovers and on their way to and from flights.

The new layout (above) brings clearer sightlines — important for both shoppers and passengers. In the previous design (below), storefronts were clearly secondary to airport architecture.

Gone are the days of a utilitarian facade for the concessions. Now, every surface enhances design.

MAJOR TENANTS

NAME	TYPE	GLA (SQ. FT.)
Johnston & Murphy	Shoestore	818
Wilson's Leather	Leather goods	1,241
Liz Claiborne	Apparel	1,489
Discovery Store	Gifts	1,344
Lands' End	Apparel	1,310

Local retailers (below) provide a last chance to pick up souvenirs on the way home.

The existing retail concourse was a congested, utilitarian space with unimaginative storefronts. It lacked any sense of a retail environment. The design goal of the redevelopment was to revitalize the passenger amenities and increase the profitability of the concessions. Airport management picked a designer, Architectural Alliance, that had two seemingly unrelated studios: retail design and aviation architecture. Customer demographics were highly favorable: an average of 80,000 passengers walk through the airport each day; they have an average annual income between $60,000 and $70,000.

Redevelopment included the removal of the freestanding retail islands, which improved sight lines and passenger circulation. Storefronts on both sides of the concourse were expanded, and the food/beverage tenants were relocated into a new food court, reclaimed from underutilized space.

Custom light sconces and chandeliers, new perforated ceiling finishes, light-colored natural materials, custom signage and specialty components transformed the airport into a distinctly retail environment. New terrazzo floors contain geographically inspired medallion artwork by Minnesota artists.

Photo: Lami-Grubb Architects

Clutter and dimness (left) gave way to light, spacious passageways (below).

A tenant criteria handbook was written to enhance the concept of a retail street. Storefront criteria promoted a distinct tenant image and three-dimensional signage projection. Tenants were encouraged to stretch the limits of the criteria to bring about an animated streetscape of storefronts complementing the new common area design.

Work took place in five phases, to ensure a full range of services and food/beverage options throughout construction. Temporary concession merchandising units were positioned in front of the construction barricades to bridge the gap during remodeling.

By the time of its completion in 1999, every concession at Northstar Crossing had been newly constructed or remodeled. Sales increased dramatically. The number of concessions increased from 38 to 68, and 16,000 square feet of new concessions and services were added.

With the renovation (above), the storefronts took on the look of retailers at a suburban shopping mall — an improvement over the old look (right).

Floor medallions with Minnesota themes bring a local flavor to the design of Northstar Crossing.

Owner and Management Company:

The Macerich Company
Santa Monica, California, United States

Architect:

Klipp Colussy Jenks DuBois Architects
Denver, Colorado, United States

Designer:

Communication Arts
Boulder, Colorado, United States

General Contractor:

Bayley Construction
Santa Ana, California, United States

Pacific View – Ventura

Ventura, California, United States

Gross size of center:
1,050,000 sq. ft.

Amount of space added or renovated:
800,000 sq. ft.

Gross leasable area excluding anchors:
401,000 sq. ft.

Total acreage of site:
58.8 acres

Type of center:
Super-regional center

Physical description:
Enclosed two-level mall

Location of trading area:
Suburban

Population:
- Primary trading area
  224,406

- Secondary trading area
  251,471

- Annualized percentage of shoppers anticipated to be from outside trade area
  10%

Development schedule:
- Original opening date
  April 1964

- Current expansion date
  November 15, 1999

Parking spaces:
- Present number
  3,895

- 873 parking spaces added in renovation

*T*wo dated two-anchor malls existed in the trade area of Oxnard and Ventura, California, about five miles apart: the Esplanade in Oxnard and Buenaventura Mall in Ventura. Their outdated appearance had kept them both from attracting hot retail tenants. In addition, the city governments had been embroiled in legal disputes for over a decade, forestalling any redevelopment.

It was decided to renovate and expand Buenaventura Mall into Pacific View – Ventura, which would have all four department stores from the two old malls as its anchors. The nine-phase project took place over two years and included renovating old anchor space and building new ones, constructing a new car parking structure, erecting a "good neighbor wall" to buffer the project from an adjacent residential area and creating a public plaza at the main entrance.

An old mall entrance (below, left) shows the dated design, which after two years became Pacific View – Ventura. An aerial view (above) places the dining terrace at the lower left of the structure.

MAJOR TENANTS		
NAME	**TYPE**	**GLA (SQ. FT.)**
Macy's	Department store	180,000
Sears	Department store	179,000
Robinson's-May	Department store	165,000
JC Penney	Department store	125,000

A bold tower and a water feature welcome shoppers at the main entrance (top). Wave-like graphics at an entrance sign (above) are part of the seaside imagery promoting the new mall. Sight lines are crisp and clear in the mall's interior (left).

The center remained operational during the entire redevelopment. As the existing center was torn down and rebuilt in two phases, a pedestrian tunnel was installed between JC Penney and the center court, and another between the center court and Macy's. To encourage customers to use these walkways, they were brightly lit and signed with a colorful graphics program. View windows were installed near the floor and at five feet to give children and adults good views of the construction. Demolition and construction over and adjacent to the tunnel were restricted to non-operating mall hours.

Views of the old mall (above, left) tell the need for renovation. The exciting storefronts, seating areas, landscaping and natural light all contribute to the new look.

Areas for relaxation can be as expansive as the new food court (above), or as intimate as a homelike seating area.

Redevelopment included significant sitework as the entire 58-acre site was rebuilt, including the construction of a three-level parking garage. Temporary walkways installed on the exterior were well lit and contained directional graphics to keep customer traffic flowing through the property and away from the construction areas. To maintain safety and complete the work, the development team used phasing plans showing ring road locations, temporary parking configurations, street entrances and customer access to the operating portions of the center. The key to success was constant communication between the contractors, the city of Ventura, tenants, customers and the development and operations teams.

Elegant facades for anchors (right and below) compare favorably to the outdated look of the old JC Penney store (opposite, below).

The redevelopment prompted a new name, logo and look. The mall was named Pacific View – Ventura to highlight its new feature, an outdoor dining terrace on the second level offering sunset views over the Pacific Ocean. The seaside imagery became a comprehensive interior and exterior graphics program that symbolized Pacific View – Ventura to the world.

Pacific View – Ventura got its name from the beautiful ocean vistas seen from this second-story dining terrace.

Certificate of Merit

Owner:

Old Mutual Life Assurance Company of South Africa

Cape Town, Republic of South Africa

Management Company:

Old Mutual Properties (Pty) Ltd.

Cape Town, Republic of South Africa

Architect/Designer:

Development Design Group, Inc., and LKA

Baltimore, Maryland, United States, and
Johannesburg, Guateng, Republic of South Africa

General Contractors:

Murray & Roberts
Gillis Mason

Johannesburg, Guateng, Republic of South Africa

The Zone@Rosebank

Johannesburg, Guateng, Republic of South Africa

Gross size of center:
290,520 sq. ft.

Amount of space added or renovated:
290,520 sq. ft.

Gross leasable area excluding anchors:
223,281 sq. ft.

Total acreage of site:
2.2 acres

Type of center:
Fashion/theme/festival center

Physical description:
Three-level enclosed mall

Location of trading area:
Urban

Population:
- Primary trading area
  140,000
- Secondary trading area
  132,000
- Annualized percentage of shoppers anticipated to be from outside trade area
  9%

Development schedule:
- Original opening dates
  1950s and 1960s
- Current expansion date
  June 24, 2000
- Future expansion
  No date set

Parking spaces:
- Present number
  564
- 521 parking spaces added in renovation

The exterior of The Zone@Rosebank hints at the excitement inside.

*T*he Zone@Rosebank is a redevelopment of an existing three-property retail site that was largely vacant, except for a Woolworths department store. A nearby center had become Johannesburg's premier retail destination, so the goal of the Zone's redevelopment was to win shoppers back.

The decision to create the Zone as South Africa's first urban entertainment center stemmed from the recent convergence of trendy shopping and interactive entertainment. Research clearly indicated a strong demand for interactive entertainment in retailing, particularly among the young aspirant market. As a result, 60 percent of the Zone has been devoted to entertainment.

An outdoor cafe (above) and the center court cafe (left) provide pleasant opportunities for resting and relaxing.

A view of the old mall (left) shows its age. The new exterior indicates a vast improvement.

MAJOR TENANTS

NAME	TYPE	GLA (SQ. FT.)
Woolworths	Department store	67,239
Ster Kinekor	Movie theaters	65,442
Galaxy World	Family entertainment center	27,954
Compact Disc Wherehouse	Music	9,361
Exclusive Books	Bookstore	5,046

Its design is dramatic. The Zone is dominated by a large central atrium, which ends in a glazed roof cone supported by circular arches. Special materials such as imported Italian tiles, polished aluminum storefronts and stainless steel-clad columns were used throughout the development.

A verical stainless steel truss, centrally positioned above the central staircase, leads the eye to the roof cone. The truss is topped with programmed Gobo lighting, which creates a kaleidoscope of lighting effects on the cone. Brightly colored floor tiles and multi-colored staircases lend the center a breezy, festive atmosphere. Television screens feature special promotions, fashion, music, upcoming events, sports and other popular programs.

During the renovation, sidewalks were completely refurbished. Parking has been increased by over 80 percent. The once fortress-like exterior of the center has been opened up to interact with its neighbors and the street. New trees, site furnishings and lighting were added.

Storefronts (above and below) exercised the developer's offer to stretch the limits of the design manual.

A high-tech security system ensures a pleasant and safe shopping experience. Closed-circuit TV comprising 64 cameras provides the technical backbone of the system. The TV screens are monitored around the clock, and security guards or police are called in when necessary. The Zone employs 22 guards, six of them on motorbikes at any given time.

Storefronts were individually designed based on criteria that set a high standard. A tenant coordinator and interior design review team were appointed to oversee the shopfitting process. They also created a unique design criteria document in poster format, which the developer says has since become a collectable.

Towers add visual drama to the center court area.

The cinema lobby adopts a high-tech look.

A stainless steel tower at the center court is topped by a lighting system that projects kaleidoscopic effects on the roof cone.

The opening day was yet one more first for South Africa: the multiplex cinemas premiered the same film, showing simultaneously on all 10 screens. The dominant local radio station hosted a large party, selling out all tickets three days beforehand. In addition to being a design achievement, The Zone@Rosebank has successfully pioneered the concept of entertainment retail in South Africa.

The Zone@Rosebank has successfully achieved its mission to become an interactive shopping and entertainment center.

THE FOUNDATION OF EXCELLENCE

*"Tentative efforts lead to tentative outcomes.
Therefore give yourself fully to your endeavors...
...And one day you will build something that endures.
Something worthy of your potential."*

Epictetus - 55-135 AD
Roman Teacher & Philosopher

Scottsdale Fashion Square, Scottsdale, Az.

You have a choice in this business...
We're working hard to be your best choice.

Date Due

APR 3 0 2004

BRODART, CO.   Cat. No. 23-233-003   Printed in U.S.A.